Dimples & Frowns and All My Ups & Downs

S. Zapata

Published by Bound Adventures
PO Box 4294, Arcata, CA 95518

www.instagram.com/boundadventures

Cover design by Kat Savage

Editing by Andrea Delangis

Dedicated to those
who think this is about them...

And to the one person who made me realize
I could love again after having my heart
shattered into a million pieces.

I will always be forever indebted to you.

And I will always love you.

Dimples

Your Voice

I could listen
to your deep voice all day,
lulling me in
Your dimples deep and
teasing,
our fingers intertwined.
Your eyes like
pools of chocolate
I could drown in.
This isn't me, that isn't you.

Another time, another place
would things have been
different?
I cannot explain
what I see in you,
I cannot explain
the comfort I feel
when I am with you.
I cannot explain any of it…

So I won't.

This Isn't

this isn't me
this girl,
who cries incessantly
this isn't me
who doesn't dare to dream

this isn't you
the boy who doesn't smile,
this isn't you
who cannot crack a joke

this isn't us
broken and waiting,
this isn't us
destroyed and hating

this isn't me
this isn't you
this isn't us…

…what do we do?

Run

I want to run away to somewhere
I don't know.
I want to leave
everything behind
and start over somewhere new.
Where no one knows me,
not even myself.

I want to burn everything to
the ground.
There is nothing
left for me here.

I want to run away to somewhere
I have never been,
But I have nowhere to go.

Not Alone

Your eyes
like pools of emeralds
I melt whenever
I stare into them.
The depths speak volumes
of pain endured & love lost.
I want to reach out
to touch your face,
to stroke your cheek
with a trace of my lips.
My pain recognizes yours,
calls to me,
pulls me forward.
My heart stutters to a stop
at the gentle kiss
you press to my lips.
Fingers search and find,
intertwine with yours.
I breathe you in
like my life depends on it.
Your free hand reaches
to the nape of my neck,
searches under my
thick locks of hair
for the back of my neck.

You grasp me,
pull me closer.
The length of our bodies
pressed so tightly
I can feel you breathe.
I can feel your heart beat
I can feel you…
Your lips on mine
turn rough,
your desperation matched
and surpassed by my own.
I cannot breathe
I don't want to
I need this escape
like my life depends on it…

…and maybe it does.

We separate,
a silent moan
shared between us
in the night air.
I don't want to breathe,
don't dare.
Our fingers
tightly intertwined,
Still, the distance
between us

suddenly too far,
even though
we are still together,
still touch.
The forbidden
hangs above us,
not a word spoken
silence, like fog, descends.
Maybe it is enough to know
we are not alone.

I Want You

Your words
are hollow and broken.
I sit by your side and listen
to the pieces of your heart
shatter
and clatter
to the ground.
I tell you it will get better.
I gently dry your tears
I want to relieve your fears.
I want so much
to take away the pain.
to put the pieces of your heart
back together
and love them forever.
You don't see me that way
though,
so off on the sidelines I stay.
I want you, oh how I want you,
And you…you
don't want me that way.

I Won't Ask

I won't ask for the stars
because I know you can't
reach them.

I only ask to love
and to be loved in return.

I Would Rather

I would rather stare
into your eyes
than look at the stars,
I would rather hear the sound
of your voice
than steel string guitars,
I would rather
we were forced to part
than to never have felt the
beating of your heart.

Despite all this
unbearable pain,
all of this unwanted disdain
I would rather endure,
this moment of pure.

I would rather have loved you,
and never been loved back.
I would rather we never met,
then I wouldn't know
what I lacked.

Supposed to Be

What if the reason
    I cannot think about a
    future without you,
Is because I am not meant to?
I cannot think
    of another route,
because that is not
    what it is about.

Maybe what I am supposed to do,
is eventually
wind up with you.

Together

what if this pain
that feels like forever,
is really meant to show us
that we are meant to be
together?

Phoenix

Flames only burn you
if you let them lick you

Smoke only steals
your breath
if you allow it
to smother you

Ash only singes you
if you reach out
and touch it

And a Phoenix only flies
if you
spread
your
wings...

To Love

To err is to be human,
but to love, ah, to love
is to have lived

Got it Bad

"You've got it bad,"
they say
"You'll never be the same."
They tell me that
they are happy for me
like it is some
kind of game.
They talk about forevers
& the happily ever afters.
I imagine the nights
& all the soft laughter.

We know
this cannot last forever
we cannot be together.
We are only here
to comfort each other on
dark nights
and that does not
equate into a life.

Sweet Serenity

The calm I feel with you
    is like no other
my heart should be racing,
    skipping beats

But there is only happiness
    and this sweet,
    sweet serenity

Indubitably

I wish we could
stay like this
wrapped in
each others arms
no need for panic,
hurt or alarm.
Just simply to know
you are there
The soft touch
of your long fingers,
on my skin
the feel of your shirt
beneath my hand, so thin
I look up at you
gazing into your eyes,
chocolate-y brown
& deep as the skies
"I want us to stay
like this," I whisper
"In your arms happily."
He whispers in my ear:
"Indubitably."

I Am in Love

I am in love with a boy
whose heart has died

I am in love with a boy
who cannot be mine

Happy

I just want you
to see me
the way I see you,
I just want
to make you happy.
I see those dimples deepen
with your smile,
I watch them travel
up your face,
to your eyes,
and make them twinkle
like stars…

But how can I make
you as happy as I want?

If I do not, cannot,
make myself happy
in my own heart?

Headlong

I will run into your arms
every chance I get
every chance I am let
I will run headlong into
storms

Human Again

Sometimes all you need
is some sun, a book,
and a dog
to feel human again.

your girl

I want to be the kind of girl,
You scoop up in a hug & twirl
I want to be the last girl
With whom you've lain,
I want to be the girl
you stop to kiss in the rain.

Okay

Today I said, "Okay,
I will not fall apart
this way."
You looked at me,
& I felt myself melting.

I said that I
would be okay
I wouldn't let this crush
effect me this way,
but then I feel the pull
of you and your
intoxicating dimples

What I Really Want

I want to chase
away the sadness
in your eyes,
I want to give you
reasons to smile,
and tease you as I try to pull
out those shy little dimples.
Laugh at you
while you try to fight,
and listen to you laugh
when you are unable to.
But mostly,
I just really want to love you.

You Smile

I wait for you
to notice me.
I hang on your
every word.
When you smile at me,
I swear,
it lights up my
whole world.

Coping

Lying, naked, next to you
my lips pressed to your skin
I close my eyes,
breathe you in.
This calm I feel
nothing can undo

I run my fingers
across your shoulder
Trace each petal
of your edelweiss
Each time you hold me close,
Another part of me dies.
I want to feel braver,
I want to feel bolder.

But the words that I say
In the darkness of your room,
Secluded among
your sheets of blue,
is the only time
I feel so brave.

For only here
can we really talk

About our hopes and dreams,
about yours and my
true feelings.
Out in the open we both balk.

How is it that we can be so open
And yet be so quick to shy away
When everything hits
the light of day?
I guess that's just
our way of coping.

Dreaming

Love is falling asleep
next to you,
and still dreaming
of you all night.

Crushing

just when I think my crush
on you might leave,
you walk in
& I can no longer breathe.

Reach Out to Me

There are days
I pretend I don't care,
those thoughts vanish when
you run your fingers
through my hair.
The days I pretend
you aren't what I need,
you reach out to me
and it makes
my heart bleed.

What I See

I wish you could see you,
the way I see you
your mischievous grin
your happy soul,
the one you hide away
to never come out and play.
If I am lucky
you let me see
that side of you.
I just don't understand
how you can't,
how you don't realize,
its this person I idolize.
This is the reason
I want you so bad,
but you don't see you
the way I do.
So this will always be
the best I ever had.

Sometimes

Sometimes all you need,
is a puppy's nose
at your feet.

Summer

a mid-summers dream
the sun, the heat
the smell of sunscreen
on your sun-baked skin
evenings of the hum
of lawnmowers at work
the chorus of frogs
at twilight
leave the window open
to feel the cool air on my skin
and to stare out at my dreams
reflected in the summer stars

Kiss Me

Kiss me
in the Spring
among the soft rain
of cherry blossoms

Kiss me in the Summer
splashing in the cold water
of the river

Kiss me in the Fall
among the cascade of leaves
red, yellow & gold

Kiss me in the Winter
amid the raindrops
in the middle of the street

Kiss me & show me love
and I will show you
all the seasons

Lost Forever

Your eyes like
pools of chocolate
Your dimples like caverns
I want to get lost in.
Your touch like
stardust on my skin
Your lips like
candied apples.
Your love so consuming
Your heart lost forever…
…never to be mine.

Nobody

Nobody sings
at the top of their lungs,
like those in love
or those
whose heart has been broken.

It All Fades Away

You whisper in my ear,
the things I want to hear
tell me everything I want,
all the possibilities
you flaunt.
When daylight comes,
the soberness shuns
& it all fades away
like dreams,
never what it seems.

Limited Time

The daylight steals
what the nighttime reveals

I am yours and you are mine
but only for a limited time

You Tell Me

You tell me this cannot be,
but here you are in bed
with me.
You tell me it's me
you will miss,
but it's me in the darkness
you kiss.
I shouldn't have ever
let myself fall,
but I would rather have you
in the darkness,
than not at all.

Give You the World

sweet little kisses
dusting my nose
that's how your love shows.
Murmur to me
that I am "your girl"
and I will give you
the whole damn world.

Poetry Dreams

Deep breaths beside me
as you lay satiated
from our love-making,
while I lie here denying
what the morning brings,
and write sweet,
poetic dreams.

What We Want

You say that we mustn't,
        but you cannot stop
it's not just what we need,
     it's what we both want.

you tell me you never snuggle,
so why is it that your arm,
is wrapped, tightly around me
as the soft sleep
of your breath
brushes my neck?

My Boy

You are in my thoughts,
in my heart
no matter what it seems.
I tell you I am here,
no matter what.
Even if my heart
suffers the cut,
of my hope dying
ever so slow.
You will always
be my boy.

So Madly

I am so madly,
    deeply,
    insanely,
in love with you.

That is all.

Frowns

Your Daggers

Your words like daggers,
they cut me
you turn your back & leave,
I say finally.
You kick me to the ground;
I say thank you
as I fall down.
You shouldn't have
this affect over
the world I see.
You shouldn't have
this affect over me.
You cut me until I bleed,
but for more, I will always
beg & plead.
It is never enough
all that I do,
my love is never
enough for you.
You laugh and point out
my shame
you curse & mock my pain,
my illness
has become your disease.
no matter how much

of this nightmare
I attempt to ease.
I cannot stop you as you go,
my screams are hollow,
you don't hear my "no".
I would have done anything
to fix this,
I would have done anything
for one more kiss.
How has this become my fault?
When it is you who caused
my heart to halt?
Your words like daggers
they cut me
I turn my back & leave…
…finally…

Drowning

The pain surrounds me,
I am drowning
in a pit of despair.
All around me the world
keeps turning,
as if they do not know,
as if they do not care.
They just continue on
it makes me want to scream
it seems so unfair,
that while I drown my sorrow,
they just continue
on their way.

Seasons

Happy…
…time flies
Sadness…
…time cries
You cannot grasp it,
when you are so
happy and content.
Or it crawls like a spider with
knives for legs
when pain and sorrow has
your heart all in a daze.

Our Escape

There's a stack of books
beside his bed
laying there waiting
to be read.
There is a calendar pinned
to the wall in his room,
stuck on the month of May,
stuck in gloom.
The sheets are a tangled,
messed up ball,
no words are spoken.
Both hearts, equally broken.

This is where we come
to fall apart.
This is where we try to mend
the breaking of our hearts.
This is where we try
to run away,
This is where
there is nothing left to say.

We hold each other in our
grief,
We hold each other though our
time together is brief.
We are both aching, hurt and
lost.

There is no escaping, this
pain always endures.
There is only this momentary
relief that lures.
There is only the sound of his
breath in my ear.
There is only us trying to mask
our fear.

Sometimes there is this
sweet relief,
other times we are too
depressed to leave.
There are times our tears
take over,
when the hurt comes in waves
and neither of us
can handle the days.
We escape to a room
to smother our gloom,

both trying to feel something
besides this horrendous pain

Whisper

Whisper in my ear
that you like me

Whisper in my ear
that you need me

Whisper in my ear
that you want me

Whisper in my ear
that you love me

Whisper in my ear…

…I won't believe you anyways

Little Red Royal

My typewriter
is my confessional,
it gives voice to words
I cannot say,
bringing comfort
in the tick of the keys.

Words flowing through
my fingertips,
freeing my soul
with each letter,
its my solitary therapy.

Allowing my brain to free flow
these poisonous thoughts
away,
leaves me feeling lighter
every day.

These thoughts will kill me
if I do not set them free,
sitting here with my coffee
and my little, red Royal.

Little Less

I hope some day
it hurts a little less.
I hope some day,
my eyes will not
be so red and puffy.
I hope some day
these dreams will let me
sleep.

I hope my mind will let me
rest.
I hope my mind
will give me peace,
I hope my mind
will stop reliving
the moment you said goodbye.

I hope some day my heart
will be patched back
together,
and I won't be able to feel.
I hope each day
I miss you a little less.

Glass Houses

People in glass houses
shouldn't throw stones,
or look down their noses
from their lofty thrones.
Who are you to determine
wrong from right?
Who are you to want
to start a fight?
What pleasure do you receive
by starting rumors
& causing hearts to bleed?
I guess the bigger person
is I,
who witnesses big secrets
and lets them lie.
Like a high school mean girl,
you spread rumors
to build up your throne
Oh, but you forget:
people in glass homes
should never,
ever,
throw stones.

Okay

"Are you okay?"
they ask

I don't even know
what 'okay' is
any more

Truth Lies

fingers intertwined
hand soft and caring
eyes staring
hot and daring

whisper to me that everything
will be okay
that I can make it
through the day
that you will be there every
step of the way

kiss me
lips soft to the touch
the gentle caress not rushed
hands soft brush

can't breathe
open my eyes
truth lies
and the dream dies

Whole

My fingers type
what my soul writes.
The pain relieves
as it leaves,
me broken and bound
half drowned
in tears that won't subside.
In pain that will not hide.
I am ripped open,
left completely broken.
Tell me tomorrow
will be better,
and I am bound to take
another header
down this dark hole of my life.
Drowning in my pain and
strife.
Take these broken words from
my soul
help me feel human, help me
feel whole.

Since You Left

Have you ever held
a grain of sand
in your hand?
And wondered at the magic
it held?

And then the wind picked up
and that grain of sand
was gone?

Too small, lost
in a big empty world.

That has been my life
since you left.

Not Enough

I don't understand
how all this time can go by?
Now, suddenly,
you turn a blind eye.
Why did you choose
to tear us apart?
Did you feel this way
from the start?
I tried to do all that I could,
and all that I should,
to keep this love alive.
I did not think
it would ever die.
Tell me when did you know,
that you wanted to go?
That you wanted to
gather your stuff?
That my love wasn't enough?

Why wasn't it enough?

Why

It isn't the heart breaking
that hurts the most,
it is the constant question in
your head:
'Why?'

'Why did this happen?'
'Why am I not good enough?'

'Why?'

That question
will eat you alive.

Fall

I wish we hadn't broken up
at all
I wish it hadn't happened
in Fall.
Fall is…
was…
my favorite season.
And now there is no reason,
at all,
for it to be
my favorite season.

I Hide

I hide in my darkness
because it is familiar.
A home I begrudgingly allow
to suck everything from me.

I hide behind my anxiety
because it consumes me,
no one will like me
and my aggressive tendencies.

I hide behind my anger
because it fuels
my will to live.
Despite the fact
that everything
is against me.

I rise somehow
with these burdens.
A soldier among flames.
Battles scar my body.
My heart no longer bleeds,
I died long ago, inside.

Cannot Be Trusted

Every time I start to feel
a modicum of happiness
the doubt starts to creep in
like I cannot be trusted
to be
Happy

Faking

sometimes it frightens
even me
how good I am
at faking being happy

The Trading Game

Only be ready for happiness
if you are willing to
trade it for sadness.
The one does not travel
without the other
and both,
in their own way,
smother.

Promises

People will promise
whatever you want to hear.
Give you promises,
for anything far or near.

When it comes time
to follow through,
they will always abandon you.

Cry

I cannot believe
you can sit here
& watch
me cry

While you harshly,
blatantly,
boldy,
lie

Despair

I push you away
in hopes you will stay.
I don't know how
that makes sense?
I just want to know
you love me.
And you will always
stay with me
And that, my darling, is where
I keep falling into
my pit of despair.

Thrown Away

I send you old pictures &
Facebook memories
because I want you
to feel the same pain
I feel when I see them.
I want to remind you
of what you threw away.
I want you to read the things
I wrote about you,
blinded in my love.
I want to make you cry,
like every day I see these.
I just want you to realize
what you threw away.

Drown

I still have feelings for him
Even though I try to tap
them down
For if I don't
I will most surely drown.

Death of Me

It is hard to explain a crush
that breaks your heart.
That makes you forget
what its like to breathe,
to forget how to stare
into anything
but those eyes.
Kiss anything
but those glorious dimples
carved into your cheeks.

This crush I have on you
Will surely be the death of me.

When You Care

The days you reach for me
when you say you need me,
I would give anything to stay
there
in that moment when I feel you
care.
When you bring me close to you
feel the rhythm of your heart
pound in you,
I realize that no matter
how I deny it,
or how much I try to fight it,
I completely melt into you.
You are all that I want to do
I want to be yours
& you to be mine
But I don't know that there
Will ever be
An "our time"

Not Around

If ever there was a time
when I need you around,
it would be now.

But you aren't around.
You aren't mine
so I remain here,
repeating over and over:

"I am fine."

Bruises

Bruises from within,
bruises from inside,
bruises I try to hide.

They fill up my soul,
burst through my skin,
I cannot hold them in.

People think I am clumsy,
I just let them think
they are right.

But really they are just
from a cruel life.

I Want to, But...

I want to trust,
but I have been burned too many
times
I want to believe,
but I have been proven wrong
too many times
I want to have
self-confidence,
but my soul has been beaten
I want to have self-esteem,
but I have always been told I
am ugly
I want affection,
but cannot stand to be touched
I want to be loved,
but I don't know what love is
anymore

She Thinks

She thinks,
love is a late night booty
call.
She thinks,
two times is enough before
they fall.
She doesn't
believe in love.
She thinks,
her broken past is something
to hide.
Don't tell her
you think she is beautiful.
She will point out
all the things she thinks make
her dull.
Her brokenness,
that she thinks makes her
unwanted
is exactly
why her admirers feel daunted
Her soul is dark & shattered
and in the end,
that's all that mattered.

I Fight

I fight to move on
ignore what I hear,
I am working all day
and night long
just so I can forget you,
my dear.
Walk away from me
leave me here,
I will never be able to see
what I don't want to in the
mirror.
I will never be over you,
and there is nothing I can do.

Another Piece

Laying next to you
listening to your gentle,
peaceful breaths
you fill my head
with a beautiful mess
of poetry and lies,
and another piece of me
dies

All My
Ups &
Downs

My Lie

I know when I am being lied to,
It is like when I look in the
mirror & say:
"Everything is going to be
okay."

Old Royal

Hear the clack of my old
Royal keys
as I type out this poem
on my knees.
In my new room with a view
with nothing better to do;
than type out my thoughts
and delve into the deepest of
my heart.

Words healing
my aching soul,
taking on the hardest role
of living with
grief and loss,
of doling out life's
greatest cost.

Let these words set me free,
let the pain I feel
let me be.
Allow me to move on
From this moment,
let my heart from my body

be rent,
as I fall to my knees
and force the clack from my
old Royal's keys.

Numb

The pain soaks into my soul
  My skin is cold
    I feel everything
      I feel nothing
        I am numb
          I cannot move

I cannot breathe
My chest hurts with every
attempt

The Colors of My Love

Red, black and white,
used to be the colors
of my delight.
Now they mark
the pain and sorrow,
that I had not known was
hiding in my tomorrow.
I did not see
what was ahead,
prancing around soaked
in my love of red.
I thought I felt all
the friendship of black
that I had no idea
We lacked,
I did not see
my impending fright,
standing next to you
in my dress of pure white.
Now these have become the
colors of my dread:
white, black and red

Pedestal

I put you on a pedestal
for all the world to see,
that I belonged to you
and you to me.
All the while,
I was mesmerized by
your smile,
people were concerned about
the way you spoke.
About the bad jokes and harsh
prods and pokes.
I was oblivious to everything
in your shadow,
I did everything and anything
for you.
There was never anything I
wouldn't do,
I never thought there was an
end in sight,
so when you said we were done
it took me by surprise,
I was numb.
My world fell out from under
me.

I was lost
with nowhere to go and
nothing to do,
I put you on a pedestal
for all the world to see;

All you did
was look down on me.

Orphan

I tell people I am an orphan
because it hurts less
than the truth,
it hurts less
than being unwanted.

Panic Attack

Anxiety
    heart racing
    chest crushing

Cannot breathe
    vision dimming
    world spinning

Panic

Never

I never believed in true love
or love at first sight.
Until I met him.

I never believed
someone could steal
your breath and your heart.
Until I met him.

I never believed
chores and errands
could turn into daytime
adventures.
Until I met him.

I never knew the sun
could be out,
and yet not be shining
at all.
Until I met him.

I never knew you could be alive
and yet unable to breathe.
Until I met him.

I never hated love
until it stole
everything from me.
Until he left me.

Anxiety, Depression & Me

Bad days:
    heart pounding, racing
    unable to breathe
    vision and hearing dimming
    dark storm clouds overhead
    hide away

Good days:
    hyper, excitement
    fast talking, hands waving
    jokes and life of the party
    spontaneous adventure
    let's go

One always follows the other
    yin with yang

My anxiety, depression and me

What is Joy?

"What is joy?" they ask me
"Fleeting," I respond.
"It is there, and then gone
before you know it.
Haunting like a dream.
Such happiness
that you forget
the sadness
that brought you there."
They call me a cynic,
Tell me its not all bad.
That's easy for them to say
they didn't lose
the best they had.

Tell me joy is in the sunshine
and I will describe
the rain clouds overhead.
Tell me it will get better
and I will show you the scars.
"What is joy?" you ask me
"It left when you left me."

How Can I

How can I smile
with tears in my eyes?
How can I move on,
when I can't say goodbye?
The love you once had for me,
still has a hold on me.
I cannot escape,
this unexpected fate.
How do you move on
when everything is gone?
I am destined to remain
faced with the blame
of a love that's lost hold
of a love that's gone cold.
How can I smile
when I cannot move on?

Gone

The silence burns my ears
as they strain to hear you.
Any sound,
any evidence,
that you might still be around
that you might still care.

There are no footsteps,
there is no laugh
there is no one calling out my
name…

You are gone.

Care

I have no right to care
as much as I do,
two hearts
damaged beyond repair.

So why is it
my thoughts turn to you?
When I am alone, I find myself
hoping, wishing,
Thinking of you.

I never meant
to let my heart get involved
with our physical affair,
but now I think of you
when we part.

My soul has been damaged,
beyond repair.
I really, really have no right
to look into your eyes
and care.

That Way

nothing hurts more
than to not exist
to that one
Person you wished,
would see the love
in your eyes
and read through
your lies,
that you are okay
and not dreaming
all day,
that they would notice
that they are your main focus
that you wish some day
they would just look your way,
it would really be as simple
as that.

But you forget…
they don't love you
that way.

The Day

Coffee in hand
    I try to face the day
It seems so daunting
    in every way…

When

When you are young,
they want to know
what you want to be when
you grow?

When you grow
they want to know,
when you will fall
in love
and when you are
in love,
when the engagement is.

When you are married
They cannot
stop asking,
if, and when,
there will be kids of
your own.

Oh, but how silent are
their questions now,
with the judgment in
their eyes,
feeding on all the lies

Nothing but silent
           disgust,
now that it is over.

Nightmare

I was a girl
and you were my man.
My greatest joy
was to hold your hand.
I would do anything for you,
I adored you.
I was content to be the shadow
to your light,
never quite within sight.
To go un-named,
or as simply your dame.
Just like that, you are gone.
As if it had been
a dream all along.
The truth I see now,
if I dare,
is that it is
really turning more
into a nightmare.

My Fucked Up Wish

It is fucked up, I know, to say
there is the occasional day,
when I wish,
rather than us break up
you had died,
because then I would know
it wasn't your choice
to tell me goodbye

My Darkness

my darkness blinds me,
binds me
in this darkened room
I cannot move.
curtains are drawn
to the view of the unmown lawn.
I cannot get out of bed.
I am filled to capacity with
dread.
my inhibitions suffocate me.
my anxiety digs deep
depression descends over all,
like a dark cloud in Fall.
I pull covers over my head
bury down deeper in bed.
I cannot rise.
I cannot fake and lie,
that I am okay today
but tomorrow…
    tomorrow I may…

Just Friends

Tonight as we were practicing
just being friends,
I realized
how perfectly my hand
fit in your hand.
And my heart…
well, my heart
broke all over again.

Your Hand

Your hand,
when I reached for it,
felt so right.
I slipped mine in yours
and you held it tight.
It brought back
so many memories,
as you held it there.
The sea of nostalgia
was almost too much to bear.
Such a simple act
of holding and guiding
had my poor soul
beating and sighing,
and before I could realize
you dropped my hand,
and it was all over before it
began.

People think I write poetry
because it heals
the pain inside
I write because I cannot hide
all this pain I feel inside

These Words

These words do not free me
my soul is trapped
my heart is broken.
These words keep me
from completely escaping.

Bullshit

You scold & reprimand
I don't need you
to hold my hand
I know what it is like
to be alone
this place will never be home
so don't tell me what to do
don't expect me
to listen to you
stop this chauvinistic
bullshit
before I take a swing
& land a hit
I don't need you to tell me how
to live my life
this isn't my first time
dealing with pain & strife
so fuck off
with your parental desires
and watch me rise up
like a Phoenix & drown
your bullshit in fire

Abandoned

You sat me down
when I was broken
told me that people will
abandon me,
I begged you to stay
but just like everyone else,
you left without a backward
glance

Rain or Tears

The thunder rumbles
& drowns out my cries,
the wind biting & cold
blows at my hopeless lies.
I whisper to myself
over & over again
that I am okay,
struggling through
each lonely night,
& each deep, dark day.
I wish I believed these things
I tell myself,
I wish I believed
I could handle this hand
I've been dealt,
but as I stand here,
my face upturned to the sky,
I cannot tell
if it has started to rain,
or I've started to cry

This Hurt

The door has shut,
a resounding slam in my face.
I never realized how deep
this would cut.
I never knew how it felt
to be so out of place,
in a world so dark & cold.
Now I am out here all alone
no longer with someone to hold
with all these feelings
of hurt I can't condone
I knew this day would come
when this door
would finally shut
I just didn't know
how this hurt
would cut

I Tried

"I tried to love you"
he told me one night.
"I tried so hard."
I knew when I met you
that no matter how hard I fight
that our future
was always marred,
you cannot fall for someone
whose heart is already taken
and expect them
to love you back.
I didn't want it to end,
I didn't want it to be done,
but I could practically hear
my heart breaking
and now, no matter the time,
there will always
be a crack

Fine

Bruises spot my body
like cities on a map,
people ask about all of them
but I don't respond.
You see, this bruise is from
running away
from the fears in my life,
and this one is from punching
my headboard at night,
when the nightmares get me
and I cannot breathe.
This one, this one I did
trying to out-feel
another pain
one deeper in my soul,
that I cannot reach.
But to those who see
& notice these bruises on me,
I plaster on my best
made up smile,
take a deep breath
& say
"I'm just fine".

My Pain

This rain is the physical
apparition of my pain,
always there,
lingering in dreariness
it makes me run and hide.
But there is no escape
when the darkness
comes from within.

Tell Me

Tell me you want me,
when you are with her.
Call me up,
tell me I am your girl.
I shouldn't fall for this
every time,
it's just that I so badly want
you to be mine.

Regardless

The heart wants what it wants,
    regardless of the cost,
    regardless of the return,
        the crash and burn.
So why is it that its the most
        irresistible pain?

Dying

There is nothing more
depressing,
nor devastating,
than the feel
of your heart dying
when your boy
is in a relationship
with another girl

Thank You...

..to those who told me I could do
this, when I swore I couldn't. Who
helped me when I didn't want to go
on. This poetry collection is some
of the rawest emotions I have felt
in the past two chaotic years of my
life. It is here in writing for the
world to see and that is horrifying.
A special thank you to Andrea
Delangis. Not only is she the
bestest friend a girl could have,
she also took the time to edit this
book for me, and she was there to
pick me up when I thought I couldn't
finish. She also harassed me a lot
to know who the poems were about.
These poems are a work of fiction,
but that's the power of poetry,
isn't it, to connect with the words
and feel like it is about you? Stop
being so vain, it is merely
coincidence, I'm sure…

-S. Zapata

About the Author

S. Zapata started writing at a young age to escape from reality. Years later a rough patch in her life & a growing collection of antique typewriters encouraged her to delve back into her writing. She chose to take her pain out in the form of poetry on her little red Royal.

To keep up with every-thing she's working on:

www.instagram.com/boundadventures

www.facebook.com/s.zapata